THE HOGAN
MYSTIQUE

Published by:
The American Golfer, Inc.
135 East Putnam Avenue
Greenwich, Ct. 06830
203-862-9720
FAX (203)-862-9724

Distribution to the golf trade by:
The Booklegger
13100 Grass Valley Avenue
Grass Valley, CA 95945
(916)-272-1556

Distribution to the book trade by:
Triumph Books
644 S. Clark Street, Suite 2000
Chicago, IL 60605
(312)-939-3330

Design by:
NSI Design Group, Inc.
37 W. 17th Street
New York, NY 10011
(212)-206-9090

Film and separations by:
DOTS
31 East 28th Street
New York, NY 10016
(212)-779-4888

Printed by Amilcare Pizzi, Milan, Italy

ACKNOWLEDGMENTS
A special thanks to Scott Sayers, Robert
MacDonald and Bruce Smith for their help and
encouragement and also to Steve Trattner and
Barbara Gaynor of Lewis & Trattner and Bill
Hasenauer of Blazzard, Grodd & Hasenauer for
their legal guidance. And grateful appreciation
to Nancy Koch at NSI Design Group for the
terrific art direction, Belinda Butti and Steve Ku
at DOTS for the great film work and Desmond
Tolhurst for his invaluable editorial assistance.

The Hogan Mystique/The American Golfer, Inc.

ISBN 1-880141-85-X: $50.00

For Elihu Davis, the world's greatest.

THE HOGAN MYSTIQUE

Classic Photographs Of The Great Ben Hogan By Jules Alexander

"The Standards of the Man" By Dave Anderson

"The Hawk" By Ben Crenshaw

"Hogan His Ownself" By Dan Jenkins

Commentary By Ken Venturi

The American Golfer, Inc. ☐ 135 East Putnam Avenue ☐ Greenwich, CT 06830 ☐ Martin Davis, Editor & Publisher

CONTENTS

E D I T O R ' S N O T E

By Martin Davis

To serious golfers the name Ben Hogan conjures up thoughts of technical perfection in the golf swing. For generations of golfers, Hogan's golf swing has been the ultimate — the one to emulate, the standard by which all others are judged. To this day, golf's greatest teachers still use Hogan as the model.

But Ben Hogan was much more. In his heyday he was a man who dominated his sport for more than two decades in spite of tremendous physical odds. He recorded 63 victories as a professional, including at least nine majors. And in the minds of many golf aficionados, he is the preeminent striker of the ball, as well as a shot maker without peer, perhaps the greatest ever.

Ken Venturi at the 1959 Open.

But it was what his pal Jimmy Demaret called Hogan's "inside game... the unbelievable will to win, the quiet determination, the intense concentration" that truly set him apart and drove him to such great heights.

This book began simply as a collection of the wonderful black-and-white photographs that Jules Alexander took of Mr. Hogan at the 1959 U.S. Open at Winged Foot. What has evolved is a celebration of Ben Hogan featuring a collection of original essays by a virtual "Murderer's Row" of contributors: Dave Anderson, the Pulitzer Prize winning columnist from *The New York Times*; Ben Crenshaw, the 1984 Masters winner and historian of the game; and Dan Jenkins, the celebrated author and golf writer. In addition, Ken Venturi, the long-time CBS golf analyst and close friend of Mr. Hogan's, provides the running commentary accompanying the photographs.

Although this book was not intended to be an instruction book, Ken's commentary, and the photographs themselves, provide much good information of clearly an instructional nature. Incidentally, through the use of modern technology we have enhanced the black-and-white photographs so as to bring out a considerable range of detail.

We hope you enjoy the book.

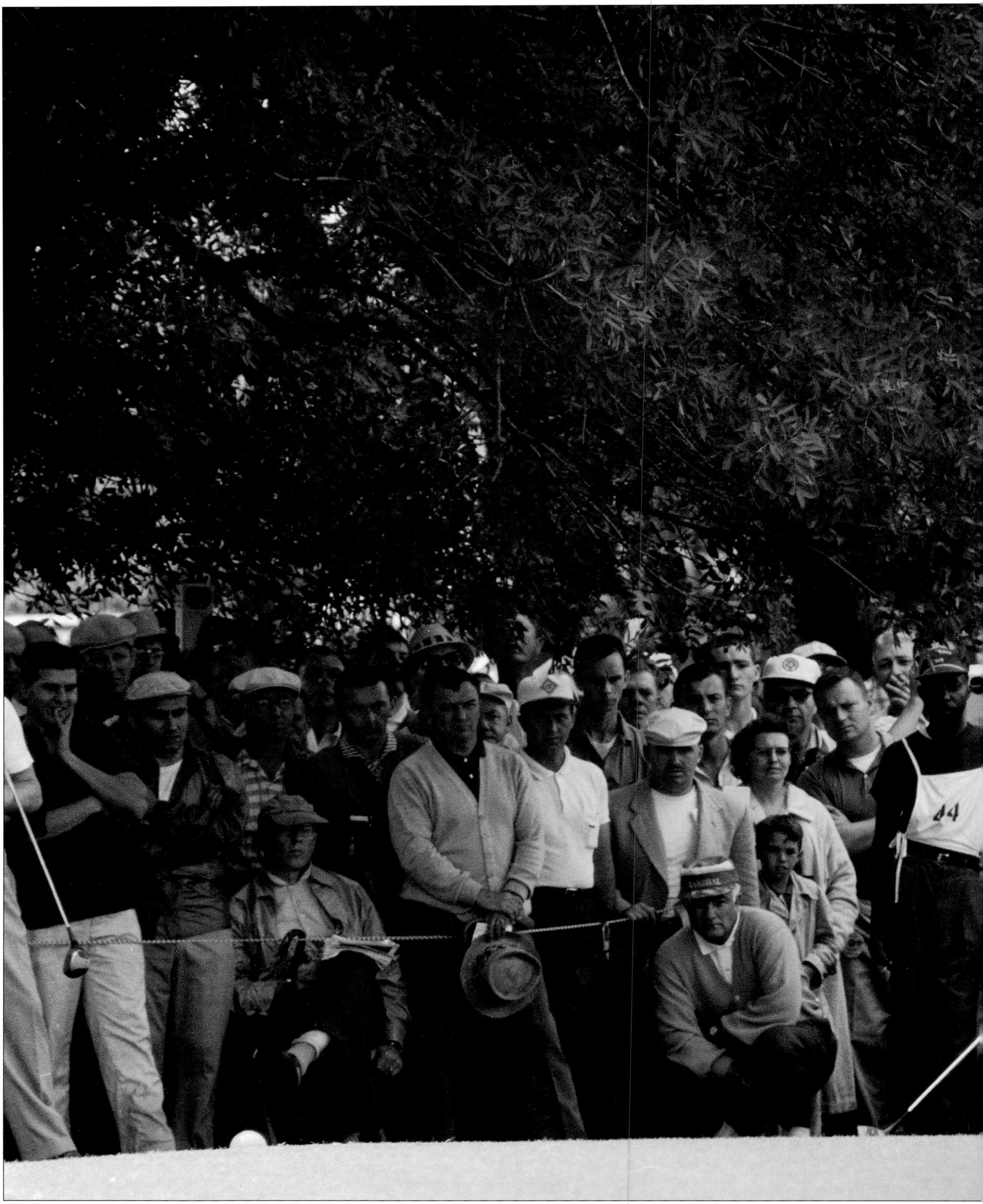
44

THE STANDARDS OF THE MAN

By Dave Anderson

Of all the golfers in all the centuries since a Scottish shepherd first three-putted, Jack Nicklaus is generally considered to be the best, but many touring pros who remember Ben Hogan disagree. That delicate difference was perhaps best defined by Tommy Bolt, who played with and against both.

"All I know is," Bolt said in his Texas twang, "I seen Nicklaus watch Hogan practice. I never seen Hogan watch Nicklaus practice."

Scratch those words in the dirt of every practice range. Because when Ben Hogan once was asked to disclose the "secret" of his swing, he said, "the secret's in the dirt," meaning a golfer had to dig a swing out of hours, days, months and years of practice. As he had.

"My greatest accomplishment" he once said, "was being able to make a living playing golf after going broke twice starting out."

Not really. His greatest accomplishment was creating a mystique that will endure as long as duffers toil to take strokes off their handicap. That mystique developed when he won the 1950 U.S. Open at Merion only 16 months after his body was crushed in his car in a head-on accident with a bus. That mystique was enhanced when he swept the 1953 Masters, U.S. Open and British Open. That mystique was magnified in later years by his reluctance to leave Fort Worth, Texas, where he lived with his wife Valerie and supervised the Hogan golf equipment factory. Told once that Nicklaus hoped to honor him at the Memorial tournament at Muirfield Village outside Columbus, Ohio, he shook his head.

"I don't want to go up there," he said, "to be eulogized."

He could be friendly and funny with some people, abrupt with others. He's been known to answer his phone with "Henny Bogan speaking." He enjoys bantering with other Shady Oaks members. When a longtime pal, having noticed him sitting in a golf cart near a tee, once asked, "You going to watch me swing," Hogan dead-panned, "Yeah, it'll give you an excuse." But one night when he listened to Gary Player inquiring over the phone from South Africa about the position of the hands at the top of the swing, Hogan asked, "What clubs are you using now?"

"Dunlop," said Player.

"Then ask Mr. Dunlop."

At his best, Ben Hogan was indeed the best player. Over a span of eight seasons from 1946 to 1953 he won nine majors: Four U.S. Opens, two Masters, two PGA Championships, one British Open.

When he discussed tournament golf, he sounded almost religious. During the 1960 U.S. Open at Cherry Hills a United States Golf Association official watched carefully as Hogan played his ball out of a water hazard without his clubhead touching the water on the backswing.

"I don't know what the gallery would've done," the official mentioned later, "if I had to call a penalty."

"You wouldn't have had to call a penalty on me," Hogan said quickly. "I would've called it on myself."

But in the years when he tuned up for the Masters by playing Seminole in Palm Beach, Florida, in friendly matches with some of his longtime pals, he would snap the cellophane on a sleeve of new balls, toss two on the grass near the markers, then tee up the other.

"If he didn't hit a good drive, he'd hit another ball," Gardner Dickinson recalled. "But if he really creased his drive, he'd turn and say, 'No mulligans today, gentlemen.'"

Like so many other touring pros of that era, Dickinson held Hogan in awe; he even wore Hogan's trademark — a flat white linen cap. Hogan's clothes fit what Herbert Warren Wind once described as "the burning frigidity of dry ice." That white cap above gunmetal eyes peering out of his mask of concentration. Slim at 5-8 1/2 and no more than 150 pounds, he wore a white, blue or tan shirt with gray, blue or tan slacks. Sometimes a gray, blue or brown cardigan sweater. Usually black or brown shoes, occasionally white shoes. Never a golf glove.

And if Ben Hogan hadn't taken a drag on a cigarette every so often during a round, he would not have been the same golfer, young or old.

Trudging on tired legs, he shot a 66 in the third round of the 1967 Masters at age 54, his last hurrah. When the Senior PGA Tour began to flourish in the early '80's, he was too old and his legs too sore to compete in tournaments again.

"But it would be marvelous," Dickinson said, "if Ben would just show up at a senior tournament and go to the cocktail party."

Dickinson should have known better. If Ben couldn't tee it up on the first hole, it never would have made much sense to him to go to the cocktail party just to trade stories with the golfers of his era. Even though he won three U.S. Opens, two Masters and a British Open within four-and-a-half years after his bus crash, he did it on legs that ached, legs that wouldn't allow him to continue to play once he realized he could no longer play anywhere near the standards he had set. Others might not have cared how well he might play as long as he played, but he did.

"I'm the sole judge," he once said, "of my standards."

More than anything else, those standards set Ben Hogan apart. When he was asked in the early '80's which of the era's golfers he would enjoy playing against, he never hesitated.

"Tom Watson," he said quickly.

Of all those young golfers out there, why Watson?

"I've beaten all the other guys."

He had never really beaten Arnold Palmer and Jack Nicklaus when those two were dominating the Masters and the U.S. Open, but he had beaten them in their younger years and that was enough. Just as he had beaten the odds created by the bus crash and earlier by his background. Not long after William Ben Hogan was born in Dublin, Texas, on August 13, 1912, his father, Chester, the local blacksmith, died. His mother Clara soon moved her sons Royal and Ben and her daughter Queenie to Fort Worth, where Ben sold newspapers until he began caddying at 12 at the Glen Garden Country Club with another youngster named Byron Nelson. He tried the PGA Tour but when he didn't win much prize money, he took a job in Oakhurst, Texas, at a nine-hole course. Returning to the Tour in 1938 he earned $380 at the Oakland Open and was on his way. He was the PGA Tour's leading money winner in 1940 (with a total of $10,655), in 1941 ($18,358) and again in 1942 ($13,143), the year he lost an 18-hole Masters playoff to Nelson. After three years in the Army Air Force, he was discharged as a lieutenant. He led the money list again with $42,556 in 1946, when he won his first of two PGA Championships, before dominating golf for the next decade and permeating it for the next half century.

Hogan, Gene Sarazen, Nicklaus and Player are the only golfers to have won all of today's major tournaments: Masters, U.S. Open, British Open and PGA Championship.

"I always outworked everybody," he once told Nick Seitz of *Golf Digest* magazine. "Work never bothered me like it bothers some people. You can outwork the best player in the world."

Do you then become the best player?

"Yes," he said. "Yes, you do."

Whether it involved his shots or his equipment, precision was always one of his standards.

At his best, Ben Hogan was indeed the best player. Over a span of eight seasons from 1946 to 1953 he won nine majors: Four U.S. Opens, two Masters, two PGA Championships, one British Open. Sam Snead would win more PGA Tour events, 81, while Nicklaus would win 70 and Palmer 60 but Hogan, who played only occasional tournaments after his bus crash, still ranks third with 63 victories. And whenever some people thought he was through, such as after the bus crash, he showed that he had only begun to play. Going into the last round of the 1952 Masters he shared the lead but staggered in with a 79 as Snead won. Around the 18th green Claude Harmon, the 1948 Masters Champion, heard voices saying, "Ben's done. His legs are gone. This is the end." That night the Harmons had dinner with the Hogans.

"Nobody mentioned the tournament," Harmon would recall, "but I could see, looking at him sideways when he was eating, what he was thinking about. He was determined not to go out of golf with a 79. He already was planning the hours and days he would spend practicing, getting himself ready for another campaign."

That 1953 campaign would prove to be not only Hogan's best, but arguably any golfer's best. Bobby Jones is remembered for his Grand Slam in 1930, winning what were then golf's four major titles: The U.S. Open, the British Open, the U.S. Amateur and the British Amateur. But the competitive level in those four events, especially the two amateur tournaments, was nowhere near the 1953 level at the Masters, the U.S. Open at Oakmont and British Open at Carnoustie in that era before graphite shafts and metal woods, before caddies were charting yardage.

"I didn't know the yardage: I didn't want to know the yardage," Hogan once said. "There are too many variables — the wind, the air density, how you're playing that day. I would remember if I had been beside a certain tree or trap or something like that and what I hit and how I played that shot. I don't think I could play by yardage."

At Carnoustie the Scots called him "the Wee Icemon." On the PGA Tour his nicknames were "Bantam Ben" and "the Hawk" but in recent decades he has been referred to, simply and almost reverently, as "Hogan." As if he deserved the utmost respect. As if a nickname was no longer proper for what this golfer had meant to the game. And just about anybody who had ever been around him had a "Hogan story" to tell.

"About all Ben ever said in a tournament," Sam Snead remembered, "was 'good luck' on the tee and 'you're away' a few times after that. But he wasn't putting on an act. That's the way he was. The year we won the World Cup at Wentworth outside London, we were teammates and he still didn't talk."

Hogan wasn't being rude; he simply didn't want his concentration interrupted. During the 1947 Masters he was paired with Claude Harmon when his longtime pal aced the 12th hole. Upon reaching the green, Harmon took his ball out of the cup. Hogan asked his caddie to remove the flagstick, then holed a birdie putt.

"I'm sure Ben was aware of my ace," Harmon said years later, "but I don't remember him saying anything. My ace didn't help him and he wasn't going to come out of his shell."

That shell thickened once he retreated to Fort Worth, then the headquarters of the Ben Hogan golf equipment company. As the chairman he supervised product design and quality control. When his first batch of clubs arrived from the factory, he ordered them junked.

"But that's $100,000 worth of clubs," somebody said.

"They're not good clubs," he said. "Throw them away."

In time, Hogan clubs were among the best in the industry. He often appeared in his own television commercials. In one he was seen in the distance, lofting 9-iron shots to the green. But before the camera rolled he had two questions for the producer.

"Do you want the ball to come in from the right or the left?" he asked. "Do you want it to back up?"

Whether it involved his shots or his equipment, precision was always one of his standards. In the days before the 1955 U.S. Open at Olympic, a shipment of new balls was placed near his locker when he returned from a practice round. One by one, he removed each ball from its carton and peered at it through a magnifying glass. Every so often he threw one of the new balls into his shag bag. At a nearby locker E. Harvie Ward, who would win the U.S. Amateur that year and the next, shook his head.

"Excuse me, Ben," he asked, "But why are you throwing away those new balls?"

"Some of them," he replied, "have a little too much paint in the dimples."

Walking off the 18th green after Saturday's final round later that week Hogan handed one of the balls without too much paint in the dimples to Joe Dey, the executive director of the United States Golf Association.

"Joe," he said, "this is for Golf House."

Hogan assumed he had won a fifth U.S. Open, breaking the record he shared with Bobby Jones and Willie Anderson before Jack Nicklaus also won four. But to some golf people, Hogan had already won a fifth U.S. Open, what was known in 1942 as the Hale America Open, a World War II substitute for the national championship. When his 271, including a 62 in the second round, defeated Jimmy Demaret and Mike Turnesa by three strokes at Ridgemoor outside Chicago, he was presented the same USGA medal awarded to U.S. Open champions before and since. And whenever Hogan was asked later if he really won five U.S. Opens, he hedged.

"I don't want to say anything," he often said, "that sounds like sour grapes."

But now, in the Olympic locker room late that Saturday afternoon, Hogan was informed that Jack Fleck, a virtually unknown pro at two municipal courses in Davenport, Iowa, was still in the hunt.

"Is Fleck," somebody asked, "good enough to tie you?"

"He must be good," Hogan said. "He uses Hogan clubs."

Several weeks earlier, Fleck had traveled to Fort Worth to obtain a full set of the new Hogan clubs. Hogan had personally let him into the factory. Now, with birdies at the 15th and 18th holes, Fleck forced an 18-hole playoff. On the first hole, Fleck was understandably nervous. His drive landed in the rough. His second plopped into a bunker. When he finally walked onto the green where Hogan was waiting, he apologized for taking so much time.

"That's all right," Hogan said. "We don't have anywhere to go."

Hogan's words relaxed Fleck, who went on to win the playoff 69 to 72. Walking off the final green Fleck turned to Hogan and said, "I can't believe it, Ben. I can't believe it." With a gracious smile Hogan congratulated him. "He played a beautiful round of golf," Hogan said minutes later. "He's a good golfer." At the presentation ceremony, Hogan announced that he would no longer be a serious tournament golfer.

"I want to become a weekend golfer," he said, "and compete just for the fun of it."

Not quite. Hogan would tee off in several more U.S. Opens, notably in 1960 at Cherry Hills when he was in contention in the final round until his wedge to the 17th green spun back into a narrow moat. But when his U.S. Open exemptions expired, he no longer filed an entry. Asked in 1963 if he resented having to qualify at age 50, he snapped, "Yes." Would he ever attempt to qualify?

"If all the players had to qualify, I'd try to qualify with them," he said. "But as a four-time champion, if I'm not qualified to play in the Open by now, I never will be."

His first U.S. Open triumph had occurred in 1948 at Riviera, already known as "Hogan's Alley" for his victo- ries there in the 1947 and 1948 Los Angeles Open. But on February 2, 1949, hours after he had lost a Phoenix Open playoff to Jimmy Demaret, he and Valerie were driving home to Fort Worth through patches of fog outside Van Horn, Texas, when a Greyhound bus, pulling out to pass a truck, suddenly loomed in their lane. Realizing that a head-on collision was unavoidable, he flung himself across Valerie to protect her.

"Merion meant the most," he once said, "because I proved I could still win."

"I just put my head down and dived across Valerie's lap." he would say later, "like I was diving into a pool of water."

That dive may have saved both their lives, but his body was battered. When he finally was examined at an El Paso hospital, nearly 120 miles from the accident, doctors found a double fracture of the pelvis, a fractured collar bone, a fractured left ankle and a chipped rib. Valerie had bruised ribs, bruised legs and a black eye.

At first, Hogan appeared to be recovering rapidly. But two weeks later he com- plained of chest pains; a blood clot had moved from his left leg into his lungs. His blood count was dangerously low. Surgery saved his life, but created circulation prob- lems in his legs. After two months in the hospital, he returned to Fort Worth by train. Two months later he was chipping and putting. By December he was playing again. In January, his legs still bandaged, he returned to Riviera for the 1950 Los Angeles Open.

"Just introduce me like you usually would," Hogan told the announcer at the first tee. "I don't want any special attention from the gallery."

He shot 73-69-69-69—280, four under par, and appeared to be the winner until Sam Snead birdied the last two holes to force an 18-hole playoff that rain delayed for a week. Snead won, 72 to 76, but Ben Hogan was back.

"I learned," he would say later, "that, thank God, I could still play pretty close to my old form."

At the 1950 U.S. Open five months later, skeptics wondered if his battered legs could cope with Merion's hills, especially during Saturday's final 36 holes. When he arrived at the 18th tee late Saturday afternoon, he needed a par 4 to tie Lloyd Mangrum and George Fazio. After a perfect drive on the 458-yard hole, he lashed a 1-iron onto the green, nearly 40 feet from the cup. Two putts. Par. Playoff. But why had he seemed to rush that second putt?

Those battered legs shortened his competitive career but somehow they had lifted him to golf's mountaintops. And just as golf so respects him, he always respected golf.

"I had to go someplace and sit down," he said. "My legs hurt like hell."

He won Sunday's 18-hole playoff with a 69 to Mangrum's 73 and Fazio's 75. For a while it appeared that Hogan's victory might be tainted when Mangrum was penalized two strokes for lifting his ball to blow a bug off it on the 16th green but Hogan's 20-foot birdie putt on the 17th confirmed his comeback.

"Merion meant the most," he once said, "because I proved I could still win."

The next year the Open was at Oakland Hills, which golf architect Robert Trent Jones had redesigned into an outdoor torture chamber. "If I had to play this course every week," Hogan said, "I'd get into another business." It had 66 new bunkers and so much thick tangled rough that Dr. Cary Middlecoff joked, "The only way to walk down these fairways is single file." Hogan opened with a six-over-par 76, "the most stupid round of golf I've ever played," he told Valerie later. But during Saturday morning's third round he moved to within two strokes of co-leaders Jimmy Demaret and South Africa's Bobby Locke. When he arrived at the 18th tee late in the afternoon he had a one-stroke lead. After a perfect drive over Trent Jones's cavernous fairway bunkers, he spun a 6-iron to within 14 feet. When his birdie putt dropped for a three-under-par 67, he had his third Open.

"I'm glad," he said firmly at the presentation ceremony, "that I brought this course, this monster, to its knees."

In the 1953 Open at Oakmont, he opened with a 67 but after Saturday morning's third round his lead had been sliced to one stroke by Snead, who would tee off about an hour after Hogan that afternoon.

"This tournament," Hogan told sportswriters during his quick clubhouse lunch, "could come down to the last three holes. That's where the real danger is, particularly if you need to go for a birdie."

By the time Hogan got to the last three holes, he knew he was leading, but not by how much. In those years, leaderboards didn't post numbers quickly. He also knew that Snead was always capable of a birdie streak.

"All you can do in a situation like that," he said later, "is try to play as well as you can, one hole at a time."

Hogan played the last three holes in par 3, birdie 3, birdie 3 for 71 and 283, five under par, for his fourth Open, his third in four years, his fourth in six years. Then he was off to Carnoustie for his only British Open, which he won with a 68 in the final round. But he didn't bother to visit nearby St. Andrews.

"I didn't have time," he explained. "I was there for one purpose."

In retrospect, historians have wondered why Hogan didn't try to win that year's PGA Championship at Birmingham CC outside Detroit in a bid to complete a grand slam. But he never filled out a PGA entry form. Unlike recent years, when the PGA has been played three or four weeks after the British Open, the dates overlapped that year. Even before the British Open's first round that year on Wednesday, July 8, its two days of qualifying (even for Hogan) began on Monday, the same day as the PGA's semifinal matches. He also knew that to win the PGA that year, he needed to endure an opening day of two 18-hole matches, a third-round match at 36 holes, a 36-hole quarterfinal, a 36-hole semifinal and a 36-hole final — a potential 180 holes in five days.

"My legs," he explained, "weren't strong enough."

Those battered legs shortened his competitive career but somehow they had lifted him to golf's mountaintops. And just as golf so respects him, he always respected golf. One day in Fort Worth a young mother was tutoring her six-year-old son on a par-3 course when a man in his 70's approached them.

"Young lady," Ben Hogan said, "I wish to compliment you for taking the time to teach your son golf. You will never regret this effort. Your son will learn a game he can enjoy the rest of his life."

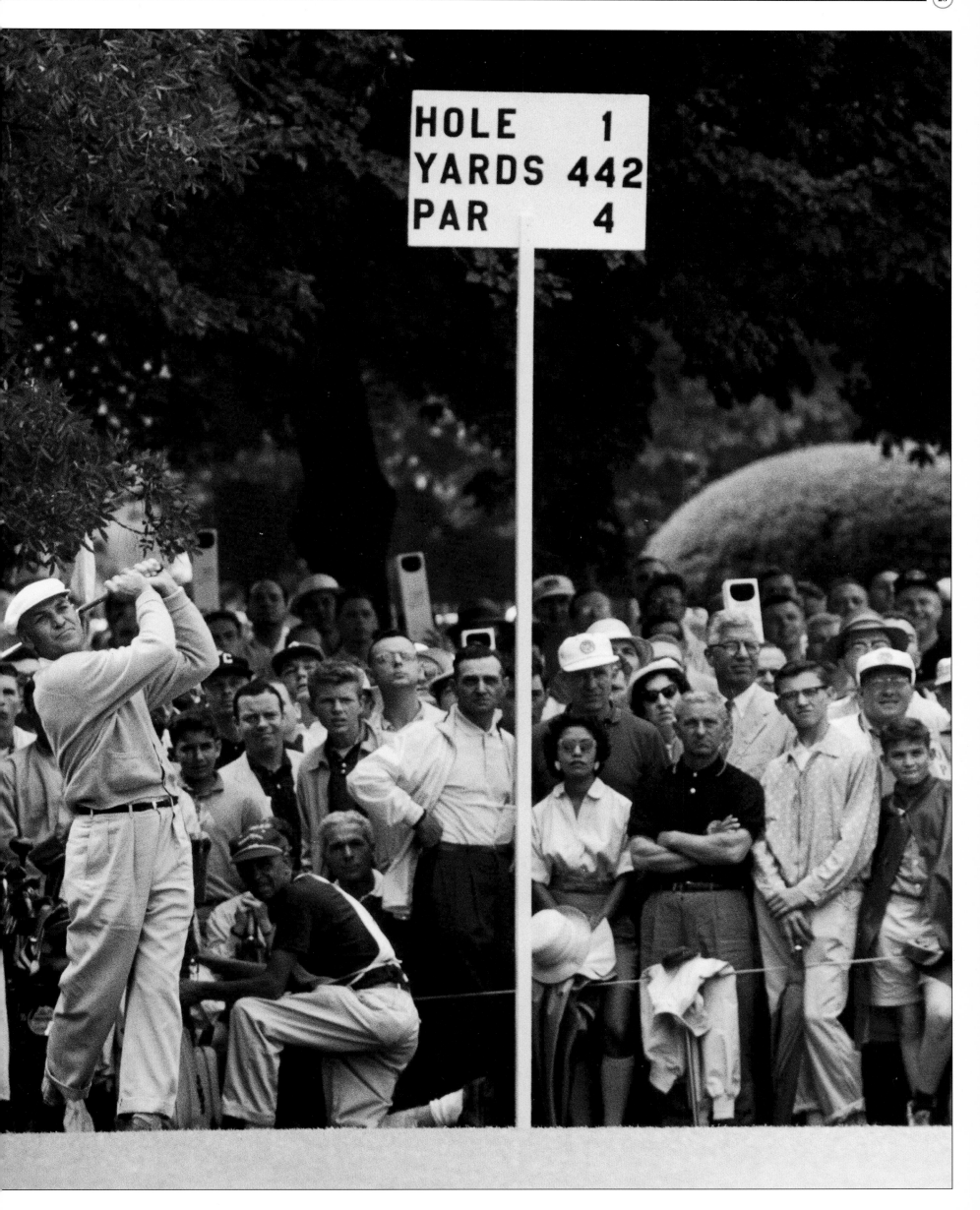

HOLE 1
YARDS 442
PAR 4

The Hawk

By Ben Crenshaw

As long as the game is played, the name Ben Hogan will always have a unique fascination for all true golfers, as well as commanding the deepest respect. For those who follow golf closely, he is the total embodiment of what a great player should be.

Jules Alexander, whose wonderful photographs of Hogan adorn these pages, told me the story of how he came by these pictures. He explained that he had been a photographer for a good many years before he attended his first big golf tournament, the 1959 U. S. Open Championship, played at Winged Foot, New York, and won by Billy Casper. His taking these pictures, he said, was truly the happiest of accidents.

Before the Open got underway on June 11, Jules went out during one of the practice rounds. He was wandering around, just enjoying the beauty of the course, when all of a sudden his eyes were attracted to a man in which many people evidently were taking a particular interest. He was conservatively dressed, of medium build and wore a distinctive white cap.

At once Jules had a special feeling about the man. "There was something fascinating about him," Jules said. "So I followed his group, and at first took just a few random shots of him. For some reason, I found myself taking more and more photos that day and also later, during the championship. In the end, I exposed many rolls of film."

The results are the photographs in this book. To me, they are the finest shots ever of Ben Hogan in action. They reflect the passion and pride of a man who truly loved his work. Especially fascinating to me are the shots that capture Hogan in a way that only a true artist, such as Jules, could possibly do.

Born in 1912, William Ben Hogan came into this world during the same year as Byron Nelson and Sam Snead, the other members of America's "Great Triumvirate." Fatherless by the age of nine, when he, his brother Royal and his mother left Dublin, Texas, for Ft. Worth, the young Ben Hogan sold newspapers, and had other jobs that probably did not interest him in the least. However, they were essential for the family to make ends meet. When he was 12 years old, he started caddying. Though he was small in comparizon to the other youngsters who gravitated toward the game, Hogan, even at that young age, soon decided to become a golfer.

...what remains burned into all our memories is the way he played and won...

I am certain that growing up in the caddie yards in those days must have been a sobering experience, one that would toughen up any young man. The older boys could make it rough on newcomers. Still, caddying then at the Glen Garden Club also had its more pleasant associations and consequences. Hogan found that he enjoyed being outdoors and watching others play the game, and the golf bug bit him, hard. He also benefited greatly from competing with another young caddie at the club, Byron Nelson. It was an amazing coincidence for two future greats to grow up together in this way, and it sustained a life-long affection between the two as well as helping both of them develop and improve their own golf games.

For the record, Hogan was not left-handed, as has been often stated. He started the game playing left-handed, because a left-handed five-iron was the only club he could acquire at the time. He was naturally right-handed and subsequently switched to the right side after he got his first set of clubs.

I am sure that Texas played a great role in the development of Hogan's game. At the time, there were some pretty tough characters in and around Ft. Worth, and they earned great fortunes in the oil fields by being bold and having a gambler's heart. This he saw, learned and absorbed. He also observed how winners at these games usually did not tip their hand. In my opinion, if you can handle the elements in Texas, you can handle them anywhere.

At first, Hogan's golf game progressed slowly. He turned professional in 1931, and twice he failed to establish himself on Tour, having to return to Ft. Worth with nothing to show for his toil. Despite lengthy practice sessions every day — a concept that his pal Jimmy Demaret swears Hogan and Nelson pioneered and brought to the Tour — he still was liable to hit low hooks that would keep him up at night and continued to torment him.

After returning home to Ft. Worth after his first try at tournament golf, Hogan made his finest move in marrying Valerie Fox. Not enough has been said of this wonderful lady, who remained undaunted by these long, lean early campaigns and the sacrifices a woman makes for a professional golfer husband. Throughout his career, they have been a perfect match.

Hogan was also fortunate in his other friends. Mr. Marvin Leonard, a wealthy department store owner in Ft. Worth, who would later build the Colonial and Shady Oaks country clubs, backed Hogan on the fledgling pro circuit and the two remained lifelong friends. Then Henry Picard, a wonderful established player, offered financial help to the Hogans at a crucial time in 1937 when they simply did not have enough money to continue on the Tour. In point of fact, they never had to take Picard up on his offer, but just knowing it was there was enough to give them a small ray of hope and sustain them until Hogan broke through in 1938.

Meanwhile, all of this time of despair and struggle was further toughening the young Hogan. People began to notice that here was a man who had an iron will and tremendous discipline and was going to battle for success like no one ever had before. He asked for and gave no quarter.

Although Hogan will always be remembered as arguably the finest ball striker ever, in my opinion his quick, analytical mind was probably his strongest personality trait as a champion golfer. He was a bit of a loner and was actually somewhat shy, but he found a great passion and love for the solitude of golf and its unique challenge.

The power of his mind made Hogan a great field marshal on the golf course. He could analyze how to play a course very rapidly, and the management of his skills and sticking to a game plan were always hallmarks of his game.

Before the 1966 U. S. Open at Olympic, young Bruce Devlin was invited to play a practice round with Hogan. Bruce had never seen the course, and in those days Olympic possessed just one fairway bunker on the left side of the sixth fairway. Not having seen any fairway bunkers on the previous holes, Bruce asked Hogan whether or not he thought the bunker was in play. Hogan replied, "No, you just hit to the right of it."

Hogan's exploits and tournament wins are well chronicled, and are laid down in hard numbers, but what remains burned into all our memories is the way he played and won them. He once was asked about today's professionals who rely heavily on yardage books in choosing a club and shot. Hogan, who preferred to play by observation, analysis and feel, said simply, "It would deprive me of the pleasure of a well-executed shot."

Often, he would walk a little distance ahead of where his tee shot had finished—

almost invariably placed in the proper quadrant of the fairway for the best angle to the green—and survey the situation for the approach shot at hand. Once he made up his mind, he would go about the preparations to play this particular shot. Without fuss came a little practice swing, followed by the set-up, a couple of waggles, and then the crack of the shot and the ball homing in on his target like a guided missile, whether that target was the pin itself or the best side of the green to putt from in a difficult situation.

It was this constant surveillance during these fact finding missions, with respect to breaking down a course and how he could best play it, that earned him the name "The Hawk." There really could not have been a more appropriate name for this man who could grab the most fearsome course by the throat and then take it apart.

Along with this intense concentration came the quality that all champions possess—unlimited patience. On one occasion at the Colonial National Invitation Tournament, Dave Marr was paired with Hogan. After some really bad breaks, Hogan double-bogied the first hole. Dave knew Hogan well enough to remark on the way to the second tee,

No one swung at a golf ball with more force or authority than Hogan. His hands were like a pair of vices...

"Gee, Ben, that's too bad about that start." Whereupon, Hogan replied, "Well, that's why they make 18 holes!" He went on to shoot a workmanlike 69, and that, I would hasten to add, was when Colonial was a much tougher course than it is today.

Hogan also took immense pride in and had the utmost respect for his profession and golf in general. With that respect came his appearance, which was polished, conservative, and tasteful. His taste in clothes closely mirrored his feelings. As he put it, "I never wanted to offend anyone."

In his tournament days, his golf shoes were custom made in England by a company by the name of Maxwell. Typical of the man, they not only looked good and fitted his taste, they had an extra spike that he liked. His trademark white cap, hand-made golf shirts and trousers with a razor sharp crease completed the highly personal look of this fabulous golfer.

At one Ben Hogan Company annual sales meeting, Hogan demonstrated the importance of a neat, thoughtful appearance. He first appeared at the meeting slightly dishevelled and with a coat and tie that did not match. He then left the room and returned in a few minutes with his customary sharp and tasteful look and said, "Let me ask you this question: Which person would you be likely to do business with?!"

A few years ago, this conservative state of mind made him a trifle impatient with the fashion of longer hair among the younger set of golfers. Nathaniel Crosby tells the story of staying with Mr. and Mrs. Hogan as houseguests of Mr. and Mrs. George Coleman. One day, Nathaniel got up early, took a shower, dressed and was returning down the hall to his bedroom when he ran into Hogan. Nathaniel had a towel in one hand and a hair dryer in another. Hogan took one look at the hair dryer and looked incredulously at Nathaniel and said, "What the hell are you gonna do with that ?!

It would be a drastic understatement to say that Hogan was and is a man of strong convictions. His word has always been rock solid.

Before the playoff for the 1950 U.S. Open at Merion between Lloyd Mangrum, George Fazio and Hogan, Ed Sullivan offered Hogan $1,000 to appear on Sullivan's "Toast of the Town" TV program on the day after the playoff. Sullivan made it clear that the offer would stand whether Hogan won or not.

Immediately after he won the playoff, Hogan received a second offer—for $1,500—to appear on another TV show. Many people would not have found it difficult to appear on both shows—Sullivan did not have an exclusive contract with Hogan--or even to take the higher offer only.

To Hogan, such actions were impossible. He appeared on Sullivan's show as agreed. The later, higher, offer was quietly refused.

As a young man, he obviously was a tireless worker who believed in a strong work ethic. But, he also loved to practice, perhaps more than any other man. Practice literally fulfilled him. His ability to analyze and develop his swing through long hours on the practice tee provided the transition from being an inveterate hooker of the ball to the success he later achieved with his patented "power fade."

In his prime, and of course for many years after, his swing—and especially his hands—were as powerful and forceful as the man himself. His set-up was so very purposeful and his posture and footwork combined with perfect balance. His no-nonsense pre-shot routine gave one the impression of total authority over the ball. Before the shot, everything about his countenance gave you the impression that the outcome would be one of total and complete submission on the part of the ball.

No one swung at a golf ball with more force or authority than Hogan. His hands were like a pair of vices that transmitted the force from his body to the ball with absolute control. His athletic and entirely functional set-up combined with the extraordinary power in his hands and forearms, legs and back to make his backward windup one immense, powerful, coiling action. His lean body would wind and wind like a machine, as the potential power built to its maximum. Then, on the downswing, he unleashed this power with such blinding hand speed that he literally smashed into the ball, hitting against his left side like no one I've seen before. To my mind, no one ever tore into the ball like Hogan.

... he was the only player I know of that younger Tour players would go out and watch...

I remember vividly the time that Lanny Wadkins and I, on a visit to Shady Oaks Country Club after our morning rounds at Colonial some years ago, watched Hogan hit some three-irons, and then some four-woods. Lanny, whom I've always thought of as one of our foremost ball strikers, and I sat spellbound, both of us amazed at the force he could generate through impact.

For me, that will be my lasting impression of Hogan, how he tore into and through each shot, with this power and force and authority and you knew the ball had to obey his command and will and streak like a laser to the target. I've never seen a ball hit like that, or heard shots that sounded like that before or since. That sound was Hogan's alone.

Two other images stand out in my mind. First, the very wide, sweeping arc of his backswing, and second, how active his hands and wrists were as he just literally burned up shot after shot, ball after ball buzzing out there on the absolutely same height and with the same boring, driving trajectory.

When I say "buzzing," I mean it. I swear, as the ball left the club on those three-irons, we could hear the ball buzz from the fantastic amount of backspin imparted by the force of the hit. Some shots, from behind, looked as if they were hit ever so slightly on the toe of the club, but I am certain this impression came from his grip being on top of the club so that, no matter how hard he swung, the clubface simply could not turn over too soon.

Jack Burke says he can still hear the sound of the club and clubshaft meeting the ball and the ground on a four-wood shot Hogan hit one day at the Masters on the fifth hole. "It went KA-whooooom!" Burke said, adding, "How he flexed that shaft into the ground!"

One year there was an exhibition at the Masters with some of the contestants trying to duplicate Gene Sarazen's double eagle 2 in 1935 on the 15th hole. Apparently, the greens were very firm that year, and Hogan hit some of the only balls that held the green with his four-wood. To make the ball come in soft and sit down on a firm green demands that you hit down and through with a slightly outside-to-in swing path and tremendous force. To make the ball stop in this situation, you have to really squeeze that ball into the turf. Hogan obviously had the shot down cold.

To a Hogan aficionado, his total ball control made him fascinating to watch on the course. Even when he was a little past his prime, he was the only player I know of that younger Tour players routinely would go out and watch—and study!—after they had finished their own rounds. It was fascinating to watch him hit irons that would land in the middle of the green and then spin left or right, as needed, toward the hole. They really couldn't hide a pin from Hogan!

Another occasion, again on the practice ground at Shady Oaks, illustrates his meticulous mind as well as his masterful approach to shotmaking. One windy day, a close friend of mine, who knew Hogan very well and played a lot of golf with him through the years, and I were watching Hogan hit balls. He banged out some six-irons and then changed to a five-iron, but kept rifling each ball with such a piercing trajectory through the wind.

Hogan stopped to rest for a minute or two, and my friend asked him, "Ben, what do you think about when you're trying to keep the ball down out of the wind?" Hogan on many occasions would think of an answer to a question by looking down at the ground for a long time—almost to the point where it would make one uncomfortable. Hogan's gears were really turning on this one, as we waited patiently for the reply. Finally, he looked up and said, "I try to hit it on the second groove."

This makes perfect sense to anyone born in Texas who learns to play in the wind!

HOGAN HIS OWNSELF

By Dan Jenkins

Anywhere around the game of golf, Ben Hogan's name rolls off the tongue the way Rembrandt's does when the subject is art. Hogan is, Hogan was, Hogan will always *be*. Talk about shelf-life.

It seems to me, looking back on it, that whenever Hogan was asked to paint us a 67 in a major — or anywhere else —the only question in his mind was whether we wanted it in oils or watercolors.

Maybe that's just my own remembrance. If so, I have excuses. It's because I have been privileged to call the man a friend all these years, to have had the honor of playing the occasional round with him when he was at his peak, and to have been lucky enough to cover many of his grandest feats.

All of that is something I sincerely treasure. It not only has given more meaning to my own sordid life as a journalist, it surely added weight to my byline in those days.

Not that I thought of it as Godzilla covers the Open. It didn't make me that arrogant at the old *Fort Worth Press*, although it did of course give me a more secure feeling than the golf writer from Food Stop, Indiana, who was covering Joe Zilch.

Over the years I've sometimes joked that if O.B. Keeler was smart enough to come from Atlanta when a guy named Jones was dominating the game, I had been just as smart in another era. I managed to get myself born and raised in Fort Worth, Texas, and grow up to find myself quite often in the presence of a guy named Hogan.

But I wouldn't want anyone to get the idea that I'm putting myself in the same category with O.B. Keeler, who traipsed after Bobby Jones on behalf of the *Atlanta Journal*. I could never have written that well in a coat and tie.

It behooves me to point out that if I was so intelligent in choosing a hometown, Ben was equally intelligent in choosing the right name. His full name is William Ben Hogan — not Benjamin, by the way. And what could William Hogan, or Bill Hogan, or Billy Hogan, have ever won?

Zip, is what I say.

No, it had to be Ben Hogan, a name that couldn't miss. Just as Babe Ruth could slam home runs, but Herman Ruth would fix your plumbing. Just as Doak Walker could dazzle you on a football field, but Ewell Walker would turn down your bank loan. Just as Ty Cobb could hit .400, but Ray Cobb would sell you insurance. Just as Sam Baugh could sling touchdown passes, but Adrian Baugh would choreograph your musical. Just as Byron Nelson, who also had the good sense to come from Fort Worth, could win golf tournaments by the truckload, but John Nelson would be the kid you can't quite remember from high school.

As we know, it is among the worst-kept secrets in golf that Ben Hogan invented practice.

Ben's name was as important as his wardrobe. Grays, tans, dark blues, white. Conservative, tasteful, well-tailored.

I have this notion that if Ben Hogan, much less Billy Hogan, had ever worn a green shirt and yellow slacks on a golf course, he couldn't have broken 85. You might as well put him in a Schlitz cap and a tank top and call him Bubba, or put him in shorts and anklets and call him Derek.

Hogan's name, incidentally, was something he valued greatly and was very protective of. Unlike today's touring pros, he would never have rented it out to any logo that came down the fairway dressed like a kitchen appliance, compact car, or fast-food franchise.

He had numerous opportunities to put his name on everything from cupcakes to vacation resorts, but he saved it for the classy golf clubs he would eventually design and manufacture.

This pride in his name was instilled in him by his mother, long before there were golfing victories. He shared this with me one day back in the 1950's when we were sitting around Colonial Country Club, his home course at the time.

As I recall, Ben was talking about someone asking him to endorse something he regarded as unworthy of him — or any other human being. He said, "I've never forgotten what my mother told me when I was a boy. She said we might not be well off, but I was as good a person as anybody else in the world."

Then with a look, he added, "Your name is the most important thing you own. Don't ever do anything to disgrace or cheapen it."

It was just a look, not *the* look. The immortalized look of The Hawk or The Wee Icemon. The look — or stare — for which Raymond Floyd was known in later years, though it did not originate with Raymond any more that it originated with Hogan, as a matter of fact.

I have seen this look in every truly great athlete or sportsman or coach I have ever encountered. Something in the eyes and *behind* the eyes. A sense of purpose, a unique dedication, a quietly fierce determination to reject failure.

Frankly, I'm not sure this look exists in many areas outside of sports. If it did, most corporate CEOs wouldn't walk splay-footed.

As we know, it is among the worst-kept secrets in golf that Ben Hogan invented practice.

The late Jimmy Demaret, who is still the game's most original wit, liked to tell about the first time he saw Hogan involved in this bizarre ritual. It happened at some tour stop on a day back before World War II. Jimmy claimed he found Ben off in a remote area of a country club, hitting a pile of balls out to a caddy standing in a patch of weeds and wildflowers.

Demaret went over to his friend and fellow Texan and asked him what in the world he was doing. When Hogan explained that he was "practicing," Demaret remarked that he couldn't possibly be practicing golf, because the course was back over there somewhere.

In the telling, Jimmy would say, "I started to call the whitesuits to come get him, but I noticed the caddy didn't have to move to pick up the five-irons he was hitting."

Trust me, I knew how fortunate I was to be able to watch Hogan practice out at Colonial in those early 1950s — him already the legend in the white cap, me the non-legend captain of the TCU golf team, but already, somehow, the golf writer for one of the two local dailies.

I recall a morning in May of 1951 when I found him hitting balls out on the 11th fairway. This was after I had gone in the pro shop as usual and said, "Where is he," and somebody had told me where to find him.

Ben only nodded at my presence out on No. 11 that day, and I didn't speak until I noticed him doing something I thought rather strange. He began to punch choked-down 3-irons about, oh, 155 yards or thereabouts.

"What the hell is *that*?" I couldn't help asking.

Without looking up, he said "I need it at Oakland Hills."

I don't remember whether he ever used a choked-down, punched 3-iron in that memorable U. S. Open, even in the final round when he shot the picture-book 67 that won it for him, but it was in the bag if he had needed it.

Preparation and repeating a swing, he liked to say, could eliminate a lot of bad luck.

Although it happened more than 40 years ago, I still look upon Ben's performance that afternoon at Oakland Hills as the greatest 18 holes of golf any mortal ever played. The reason is, he shot it on the toughest course that Joe Dey, or Robert Trent Jones, or any sane person, ever perpetrated on mankind.

As an eyewitness, let me assure you that everything you may have heard or read about Oakland Hills in '51 was true. Fairways no wider than a hotel hallway, rough almost up to the knees, deep bunkers everywhere the player stepped, and greens slicker than the top of Sam Snead's head.

...he would study each shot... as if confronted with a mathematical problem so complex only *he* could solve it. Then he would solve it with that flat, flawless swing.

Hogan's 67 may have only been three under par on the scorecard, but the average score of the field in that last round was 75, so in truth, Ben was eight-under on the evil layout — and in the pressure-packed final 18 of the National Open, thank you very much.

According to lore, this is the place where Ben supposedly said, "I brought the monster to its knees."

Actually, what I think I heard him say was something more on the order of, "I finally brought this sorry son of a monster to its knees." Something along those lines.

The fact is, Ben didn't like many golf courses, other than Colonial, Southern Hills, Seminole, Pinehurst No. 2 and what he referred to as "Riviera before the flood." Most golf courses stood between him and the Fort Worth National Bank.

In his prime in a tournament, Hogan was a fascinating study. He walked toward a green, or to his next shot in the fairway, not so much with a limp, but as if he were trudging slightly uphill. Having memorized the course, to know where not to be, he would study each shot, drawing on the ever present cigarette, as if he were confronted with a mathematical problem so complex only *he* could solve it. Then he would solve it with that flat, flawless swing.

He never acknowledged a friend in the gallery, but he would know you were there, just as he always knew that his wife, the wonderful Valerie, was always close at hand with the thermos of ice tea.

He respected the fact that there were writers like myself who had seen him play most of the round, had understood the problems he faced, and would not have to ask dumb questions later. I believe it might have been at Winged Foot in the '59 Open that he grew weary of several poets in the locker room asking him what club he had hit on the 10th, or how long his putt had been at the 6th. That's when he said to the group, "Someday a deaf mute is going to win a golf tournament and you fellows won't have anything to write about."

I have always suspected that part of Ben's inner drive stemmed from the earlier success of Byron Nelson, a kid of the same age , from the same town, a kid with whom he had caddied at Glen Garden Country Club in Fort Worth when they were teenagers.

After all, Ben was still struggling, still borrowing money twice to stay on the tour, while Byron was winning the 1937 Masters, the 1939 U.S. Open and the 1940 PGA. Three majors before Ben could get out of the box.

Moreover, it is always said by old Glen Garden members that Byron was a "more popular youngster" around the club than the shy little scuffler, Ben. And I gather it didn't do anything for Hogan's ego the day that Byron edged him one-up in an 18-hole final to win the Glen Garden caddie championship, which was certainly a major in their world back then.

But, of course if I take the position that Byron's early success may have been a factor in motivating Ben to work even harder at the game, then I suppose I have to say that Ben Crenshaw's teenage fame did the same thing for Tom Kite in Austin, that Gene Littler's quick start did as much for Billy Casper around San Diego, that Harvie Ward's rapid conquests were an influence on Ken Venturi in San Francisco, and that — I really don't have to take it all the way back to Old Tom and Young Tom, do I?

It's only guesswork, anyhow, like what was Hogan's *real* secret? I mean, apart from hitting more practice balls than anyone else in an effort to find a swing that would repeat under pressure?

I have to confess that I am a collector of Hogan stats, if not the primary curator of them.

Naturally, I contend that Ben won five U.S. Opens, which gives him one more than Bobby Jones, Jack Nicklaus and Willie Anderson. I count the "wartime" Open at Chicago's Ridgemoor in 1942. I count it because he has a gold medal for it that looks just like the ones the USGA gave him for winning at Riviera, Merion, Oakland Hills and Oakmont, and

I count it because every newspaper and radio station in America called it a major Championship at the time. Those *five* gold medals, I'm happy to say, are on display in the Hogan Trophy Room at Colonial in Fort Worth. Yep. Right there in plain sight.

I would also argue that a good many other historians would count Hogan's fifth Open if it weren't for the well-nursed memory and overly caressed record of Bobby Jones. I sometimes have the feeling that if a golfer ever does win five so-called *official* Opens, it still won't count unless he has three college degrees and a body of published literary work.

I insist as well that Hogan is the only player other than Willie Anderson to win three Opens in a row. Ben won in '48, missed '49 because of the automobile accident, then won in '50 and '51. That's three in a row that he *played in*, folks. So give it an asterisk, who'll notice?

There is another little stretch he had in the U.S. Open that I don't expect anyone will ever come close to matching. He once competed in 16 straight and never finished out of the Top Ten. It's best to show it in a chart like this:

Ben Hogan
U.S. Open 1940-1960

YEAR	EVENT	PLACE
1940	Canterbury	Tied for 5th
1941	Colonial	Tied for 3rd
1942	Ridgemoor	**WINNER**
1943	—	No Tournament (WW II)
1944	—	No Tournament (WW II)
1945	—	No Tournament (WW II)
1946	Canterbury	Tied for 4th
1947	St. Louis CC	Tied for 6th
1948	Riviera	**WINNER**
1949	Medinah	Did Not Enter (injured)
1950	Merion	**WINNER**
1951	Oakland Hills	**WINNER**
1952	Northwood	3rd
1953	Oakmont	**WINNER**
1954	Baltusrol	Tied for 6th
1955	Olympic	2nd
1956	Oak Hill	Tied for 2nd
1957	Inverness	Did Not Enter (injured)
1958	Southern Hills	Tied for 10th
1959	Winged Foot	Tied for 8th
1960	Cherry Hills	Tied for 9th

As fascinating as anything to me, statwise, are the scads of majors Ben — in his prime — never had an opportunity to play for. You can see in the chart where he missed five Opens because of the war and injuries, Opens in which he most certainly would have been the big favorite.

The British Open didn't really command his attention, for as soon as he became an established star on tour, World War II cancelled the British event for the next six years, from 1940 through 1945. In other words, had it been the major it is today, it would not have been available to him for those years. He won it, of course, the one and only time he went over to see what all the fuss was about, at Carnoustie in 1953, the year of his Triple Crown.

Again in his prime, he was denied four chances to add to his two Masters titles. That would be the three war years when it wasn't played, '43 through '45, and the year of the car wreck, '49.

When I asked him to explain the wisdom of that mysterious act, he said with a straight face, "You always overclub downwind."

His timing was just as unfortunate where the PGA Championship was concerned. Although he won the PGA twice, in 1946 and 1948, it is among the game's most startling facts, I think, that he played in it only seven times!

He competed in it from 1939 through 1942, always winning two or three matches. But then the PGA was cancelled in '43 because of the war. Hogan also missed it in '44 and '45, because he was serving in the Army Air Corps. Next came the auto accident in the winter of '49, which not only kept him out of it that year, but removed this rigorous, week-long match play competition from his schedule for the remainder of his career.

By my arithmetic, this adds up to more than 20 majors that were unavailable to him for one reason or another when he just happened to be at the top of his game. I think it's perfectly reasonable to assume that given his rate of sucess at the time — and since he was Ben Hogan — he would have won at least a third of them, and of course I must hasten to admit, as my Fort Worth blood gurgles over, that I wouldn't much care that this would drop Bobby Jones and Walter Hagen down a notch on the all-time list of major championship winners.

I still have vivid memories of some rounds of golf with Ben. Like the day at Colonial when he hit a downwind, bump-and-run 7-iron into a green, and up stiff for a birdie, when I thought the shot called for a 9-iron.

When I asked him to explain the wisdom of that mysterious act, he said with a straight face, "You always overclub downwind."

Years later, I reminded him of that moment, and got a laugh out of him by informing him that I couldn't count the number of times I'd been out of bounds over a green because I'd been overclubbing downwind ever since.

My most memorable round of golf with Hogan came on a spring day back in 1956 out at Colonial after he invited me to join him and two other players in an exhibition for the benefit of the United States Olympic Fund.

With something of a glint, he said, "You can probably swing a little faster if you try hard enough."

The other members of our foursome were Raymond Gafford, a sweet swinging club pro in town, and Ben's brother Royal, a fine local amateur. I was definitely out of place but felt a responsibility to represent all golf writers, ex-college golfers, and public-course thieves in that glamorous event.

You might imagine how surprised I was to stroll out to Colonial's first tee — a bit late, actually, and without having scooped a single practice shot — and find 5,000 people lining the first fairway. This was about 4,995 more than normally had turned out three or four years earlier to watch our matches against Baylor or Rice or even the University of Texas.

Somehow, I managed to get off the first tee with a driver without injuring myself or anyone else, but for the rest of that hole, and through the second hole, I developed a nasty habit of topping everything. My poor Titleist got into the air about as often as a croquet ball.

It was when we were walking down the third fairway that Ben came along beside me and dropped a hint that helped me make it through the rest of the round without any permanent bruises.

With something of a glint, he said, "You can probably swing a little faster if you try hard enough."

Uh-huh. The Ben Hogan I knew also had a sense of humor.

A STRAIGHTFORWARD APPROACH

Ben always said, "You never fight your eye when you look at a hole. If it looks one way, play it that way. Don't make a big deal out of an easy shot."

"It's a black and white thing. If it looks like it falls left to right, let it go left to right; if it looks like it falls right to left, let it go right to left. On a dogleg right, you don't try to hook it, on a dogleg left don't try to fade it."

When Hogan practiced at Augusta, he'd go to the right side of the old range so he could fade it around the hedges. To him, it looked like the shot called for a fade; it never looked like he could hook the ball. His swing would always follow his eye.

Ben would say "when you practice try to find the situation to fit the shot you're trying to practice. You don't go to an open field to hit draws and fades. So when you get to that position in a round, you don't have to tell your body how to do it. Your eye tells your body and builds it into it."

This was reinforced by a story that Gene Sarazen once told me. Gene said that he made two double bogies on the same hole in the U.S. Open one year and ended up losing by a shot or two. Gene told me, "I just couldn't play that hole, it just didn't fit my eye."

Hogan always said "if the hole doesn't fit your eye, create a shot — create something with a club you wouldn't ordinarily use."

■ The par-3 10th hole at Winged Foot.

ON SHOTMAKING

Hogan was rigorous in the way he approached shotmaking. For example, if you were playing the par-3 10th hole at Winged Foot with the pin on the right hand side of the green, and you hit it over the big bunker on the right with a hook and knocked it in about three feet from the hole ... as far as Hogan was concerned, you might as well find yourself another game! That's not the way it's supposed to be played. You've got to come in from the other side with a fade. That's the way it's supposed to be played! You had to play the hole with the shot the hole called for.

FOUR THEORIES

Hogan had four theories of playing and you could tell by watching him:

☐ If the pin is in the right hand side of the green, the shot goes from left to right.

☐ If the pin is in the left, it goes right to left.

☐ If the pin is in front, it goes in high.

☐ If the pin is in the back it comes in lower.

Hogan felt strongly you had to find the hole the correct way.

He always said, " You never go in high to a pin in the back, you always keep it under the hole . You never hit a full shot - a hard shot - to a pin in the back. You hit a soft lower shot to get up to it."

Hogan believed in always dropping down a club when in doubt. If you're between a 7 and an 8, take 7; between 6 and 7, take 6; between a 5 and a 4, take the 4; always drop down a club.

■ *Westchester 1970*

PREDICTABLE

Hogan was the most predictable unpre-dictable man I ever knew.

One year after a round at the Masters in the mid 1960's we were upstairs in the clubhouse. One of the long-time amateur players who was playing just ahead of Ben during the day's round came over and said, "Ben, I noticed on 13 we hit our drives to about the same spot. I hit the green with my second shot, but you laid up. How come you didn't go for it?"

Hogan replied, "Because I didn't need a three."

You never knew what he was going to say, but after he said it, you knew that's what he was going to say.

ON BEING DELIBERATE

Everything Hogan did was right hand oriented. When he talked to you, everything was done with the right hand just like he was ready to take a grip — pinkie out, two middle fingers closed. His mannerisms were so consistent.

Hogan never rushed anything. Everything was always contemplated. Everything was done in a slower manner. Nothing ever was rushed.

The only thing he did fast was swing. You couldn't make the move he made in slow motion. He had a fairly quick swing. But to make the transition of the body moving forward before his backswing was completed, it had to be done in a faster motion. This is just like Tom Watson and Nick Price. A Faldo swing, on the other hand, can be slower because it is a more of an 'arm' motion.

I think that was part of his mystique. He never answered anything fast, only if he wanted to end the conversation. Everything was calculated. He had a very definite reason why something was being done.

CONCENTRATION

Hogan deep in thought. That's typical of Hogan during a round. You don't have to look at his face to know that's Hogan, just the body language.

I don't think he could have concentrated the way he did if he didn't smoke. It gave him something to do while he was thinking. I've seen that same exact pose hundreds of times.

■ *Westchester 1970*

ON COPING WITH PRESSURE

Hogan could paint a picture in his mind and develop it with the club in his hand. He was the greatest example of coping with pressure. Whether it was for the Open or a Tour event, he created and executed the shot the same way.

THE FOUR-WOOD

Before the Masters in 1960 Hogan and I were practicing at Seminole in Florida. Ben had two four-woods in his bag and couldn't make up his mind which one he liked better. Since I needed a four-wood, I said to him, "I'll tell you what, they're both good, the one you don't want, I'll take." Hogan said, "You got it."

On the Tuesday of Masters week we were playing a practice round at Augusta and Ben had a four-wood shot to the green on the par-5 13th hole. He called me over and said, "I have to make a decision, which one of these do you like?" Knowing Hogan, I knew if I chose the one I did like, I wouldn't get it. So I chose the one I didn't want. Hogan said, "I like that one too, you can have the other one." So I ended up with the one I wanted all along.

Much later, I told Hogan the story and he said, "I got the best one!" He wouldn't admit that I got the best of him!

I still have that four-wood, but I don't carry it in my bag any more, I'm afraid I might lose it somehow — that club really means a lot to me.

MUSCLE MEMORY

Hogan strongly believed in mind over matter. He claimed there's no such thing as muscle memory. "Your muscles don't have memory," he'd say. "Your mind tells your muscles what to do."

ON PRACTICE

Ben would have practice days and he would have play days. Typically he'd arrive at the course at 9:00 A.M. and by the time he got around to hitting balls it was 10:00. He'd hit balls for two hours, have some lunch and then hit balls for three hours after lunch.

At the beginning of his practice sessions, Hogan was not concerned with accuracy, but rather with trajectory. This was one of his premier priorities. He'd say, "If you have trajectory, you can get accuracy." That's because you're striking the ball properly.

He always made a mental note of the shots he didn't hit best during a round and then work on them afterwards on the practice range. Whatever he was having trouble with, that's what would get the most attention. In any event, he'd usually go through the entire bag before finishing.

ON THE PRESS

Hogan couldn't tolerate stupid questions. Although he didn't particularly like some of the press, he didn't mind answering questions.

One year at the Masters, he had a very good round — a 67 or so. The pins were tucked and he was knocking them in tight, just missing the bunkers. This one young journalist asked him, "Mr. Hogan, you had a very good round today, but there were a lot of places where you were lucky, you barely missed the bunkers."

Hogan replied, "That's right, the more I practice the luckier I get."

Wykgyl 1957

ON HOGAN'S SET-UP

Hogan would first stand with his feet together and then take his stance. He would then fix his body for the shot it called for.

PRECISION

Hogan had a routine that didn't vary. If you look at a certain shot and he played that shot again, you could take a video and you could overlay it with the exact same moves. He was always precise, always very disciplined.

The only exception was on the 12th tee at Augusta. This was the only place where I ever saw him vary his pre-shot routine — his waggle.

If you watch the flags at the 11th and 12th holes you'll notice that when the flag is up at 11, it's down at 12. When the flag went down at 12 he would start to make his move. He would waggle three times, four times, five times.

Hogan would say, "I would never hit the ball until I felt the wind on my cheek and, therefore, the flag would be up, the wind would be consistent, it would be normal — instead of coming up or dropping down." He never wanted to catch the ball in the air when it came back up. He'd waggle long enough to catch it when it was up.

ON HIS GRIP

Why Hogan's grip looked so good — and Sam Snead's as well — is because their thumb curves back. Guys that had that little backward bow in their thumb had great grips.

THE MAXWELL SHOES

Hogan had his golf shoes custom made in England by the Maxwell Shoe Company. As you can see, Ben's shoes had an extra spike. This was a very important spike for his swing and his action because it helped keep him down through his swing and prevented slipping. You really don't see that today.

THE WAGGLE

Although Hogan is just moving into position, notice how he always keeps the club behind him. And when he waggled, he never got the sole of the club above the top of the ball. He was always waggling with the intention of hitting the ball.

Simply put, his waggle was just like his full swing, just in miniature. He never wanted to do anything in his waggle that he wouldn't do in his full swing. He never got it over the top of the ball, like some players do today.

Hogan maintained, "If you don't use it in your swing, don't use it in your waggle. Why practice something you're not going to use. Only use things that fit your golf swing."

■ *On the range — Westchester 1970*

A BASIC SWING THOUGHT

One of Hogan's fundamental swing thoughts was the elbow-to-elbow position.

He felt you should imagine a dot, about the size of a quarter, directly opposite (and inside) each elbow. When you complete your backswing, the dot on the inside of your right elbow should point directly up to the ceiling; when you swing through and complete your swing, the dot on the inside of your left elbow would be in the same position, pointing up towards the ceiling.

Simply put, when you go back, the right dot goes up, when you go through, the left dot goes up. On all of Hogan's full shots, you can clearly see it.

■ *Oakland Hills 1961*

■ *Oakland Hills 1961*

THE KNOCKOUT PUNCH

Hogan claimed the position he wanted on his backswing was the same as if he was going to throw a punch. He likened it to a prize fighter. He wanted his right hand just beside his right ear — not high over his head or behind him. From that position, just turn to the side, put the club in your hand and you'll see Hogan.

If you took the club out of his hand, he felt he could fire a blow that could knock you out!

THE ANGLE

Hogan held this angle as long as possible. If he used some of the flexible shafts of today, with the amount of force and power he generated, the shaft would flex way too much. Because of this position, he wouldn't use a shaft with a lot of flex — it had to be very stiff.

ON HIS CLUBS

No one ever played with as stiff a driver as Hogan. He had the stiffest shaft of anyone who ever played. It's hard to believe that someone could play with a driver that stiff. He played with an extra stiff steel shaft that was tipped. The first step on the shaft of his driver was just above the whipping. I never saw anything like it in my life! I tried to hit it once and it went dead right.

His irons were around a D0 to a D2 swingweight, but about D6 or 7 with the driver, a very heavy driver. On the Senior Tour today even though you're seeing longer length drivers, they're heavier too, somewhat like Ben's.

The grip on his driver was always bigger than the grips on his irons. Ben felt that he wasn't really maneuvering much with the driver - he felt that all he had to do was to hold on to it. He could create more moves with the smaller grips on his irons.

A SWING CHANGE

Hogan changed his swing when he was a terrible duck hooker. Ben felt that MacDonald Smith was the premier swinger of his day, the forerunner of all swings to copy. Ben used him as a model in developing his own swing.

He changed his swing in two fundamental ways: first, he didn't go beyond parallel in his backswing, as he had done before; and second, he changed his grip from a fairly strong one to a weaker grip.

One of the keys to Hogan's swing was his ability to move forward with his lower body, before his backswing was completed. This assured him he wouldn't hook the ball from this position. He could draw the ball from there, but not hook it.

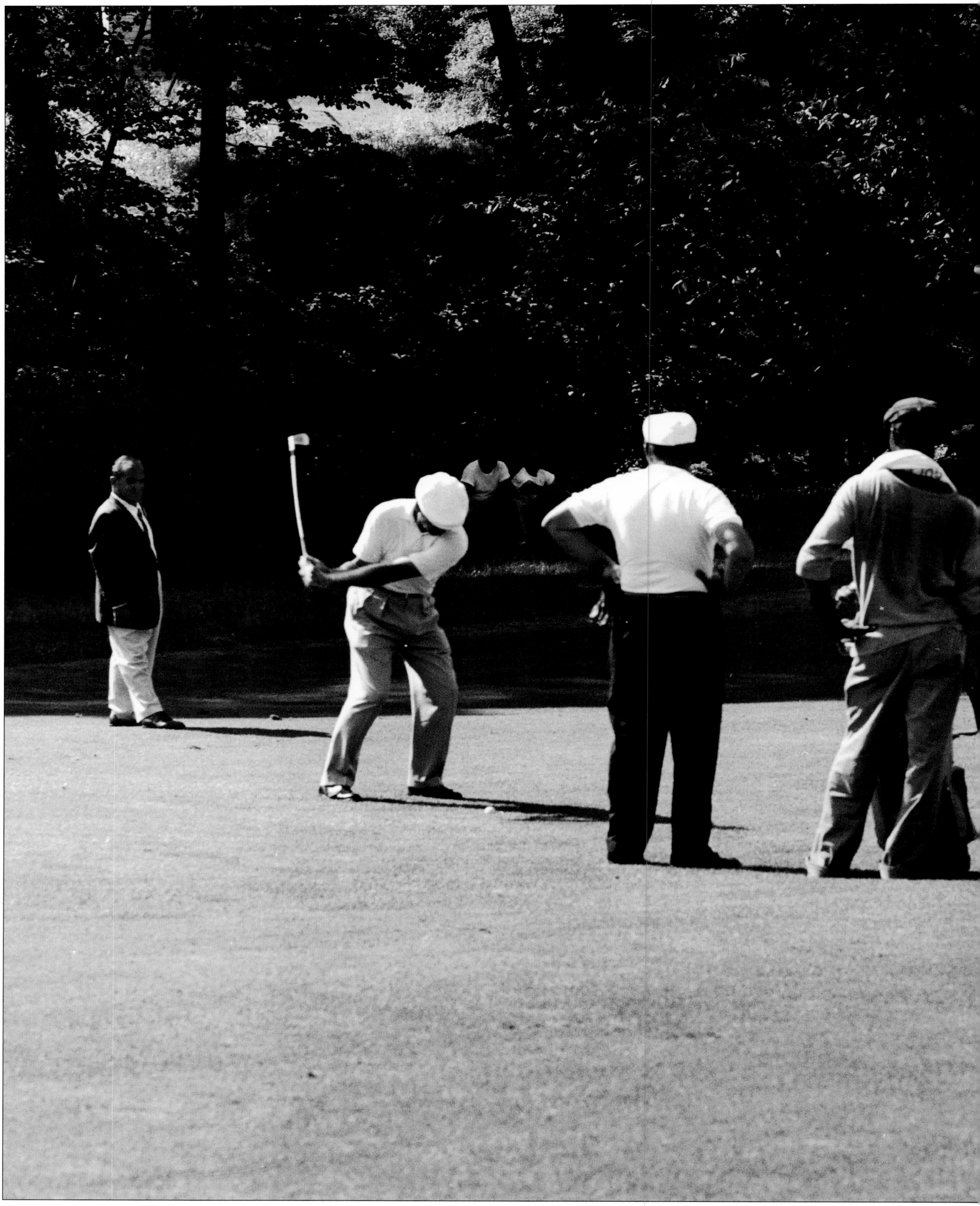

A GREAT MOVE

This is the epitome of hip position, leg flex, leg position and balance. Everything's there. If you cover his head in this picture, you wouldn't have to tell me who it is!

ON THE LEFT HAND

Hogan claimed the left hand had two functions: First, to hold on, and second, not to break down. "You don't hook a ball because you have a strong right hand," he would say. "You hook it because you have a weak left."

THE FINISH

You could tell every shot Hogan played by the way he finished it: the arm shot, the knockdown shot, the low cut shot...

You don't see that today. Every shot had a different finish — a purpose. They liked to call him a mechanical player, but he wasn't. He was *very* creative.

Here he's hitting a draw off the tee. Notice the flatter finish.

THE FIT SHOT

That's a fit shot. He's trying to fit the shot to the fairway. With a length of 376 yards, all he wants to do is put it in play.

Hogan never tried to exert himself on this type of shot, as opposed to other types of shots. It was his regular swing in slow motion.

This is a similar situation to the seventh hole at Augusta. When the greens were hard, we'd be looking for a certain area in the fairway.

A COMPARISON

These two photos provide an interesting comparison. In the photo at the left, Ben is hitting a fade with a fuller shot. Notice the extended higher finish. He's trying to hit it in higher and fade it.

Compare this with the photo above where he is playing a draw. You can tell by his move, the position of his arms, by the position of his club, by his flatter finish. Notice where the right hand has crossed over and the clubface is down.

Quite clearly, one's a draw and the other's a fade. Just note the finish.

THE HOLD SHOT

You don't see that today. That's a hold shot. Hogan seems to be saying, "It wasn't an 8-iron shot, so I'm going to arm me a little 7." You rarely see anyone out there today with that kind of talent. He's playing a little 3/4 hold shot with a 7-iron to a pin on the right. There's not a complete finish, it's a soft shot. He was masterful at this shot.

BALANCE

Carefully note how Hogan is not on his toes — he's through the shot, but his feet are still flat on the ground. Many of today's players would be much more up on their toes at this point in his swing. Also notice how much he's down, how the right knee is getting much closer to the left and how he hasn't lost any of his flex. While the left hip has cleared, nothing is spinning out, because his right shoulder and head are still lagging behind.

In order to incorporate this in his swing, Hogan would practice hitting flat-footed. He'd practice hitting the ball with seemingly no feet at all. He'd try to keep his right foot down as long as possible.

Ben was not a teacher in the conventional sense, but he could tell you how something in the golf swing felt. You'd have to ask him what it felt like when he did something. Ben could create and remember how it felt. Byron could explain how to do it. Ben would tell you how it felt.

IN COMPLETE CONTROL

Carefully note the area of the knees, the feet and their relative positions.

Very few players today remain down in this position when the club is past hip high. Most players would be high up on their toes.

This is what Ledbetter wants Faldo and Price to work on. Watch Faldo's swing and you'll see a lot of that in it.

■ Westchester 1970

■ *Oakland Hills 1961*

ON HIS SWING

Anyone who tried to copy his swing never really was successful. There was only one Hogan swing.

You could copy moves, but you were unable to copy his swing.

THE PITCH SHOT

Hogan was an excellent 'pitcher' of the ball. Almost all good low hands players are. In his full swing, Hogan didn't have the high looping hands of a Jones, his hands were much lower at the top of his backswing.

ON BUNKER PLAY

Hogan was a good bunker player —
especially if he had some green to work
with. Since he didn't have much loft on his
sand wedge, like Sam Snead or Claude
Harmon or Lloyd Mangrum, he had some
difficulty with pins cut close to the bunker
he was playing from.

■ *Editor's Note: In 1959 The Rules of Golf permitted putting while on the green with the flagstick unattended.*

ON PUTTING

Hogan was a marvelous short putter. Byron Nelson has said he would literally go weeks without missing a three-footer.

ATTENTION TO DETAIL

In his heyday, Hogan always watched everything until its end. These are typical long putt poses — he'd stay there with his putting stance until it stopped.

MOTIVATION

Hogan and I were paired together during the 1966 Open at Olympic. Midway through the round we were both on the green and Ben was away with an extremely difficult 20-foot putt. After standing over the putt for an agonizingly long period of time, he uncharacteristically walked away from it, came over to where I was standing and said in a low voice, "I can't take it back."

Now what do you say to a Ben Hogan when he says something like that?

Knowing that I had to shake him out of it, I thought for a moment and said, "Who cares? You've been beating us long enough!"

He was so mad — you could have just about seen smoke coming out of his ears. And he just about made the putt.

After our tee shots on the next hole, Hogan, walking down the fairway and looking straight ahead simply said, "Thanks." Not wanting to acknowledge what had just transpired, I replied, "For what?"

Hogan stayed so steady over the ball... it's almost like he could will them in.

As long as I can recall, Hogan used a center-shafted putter that was flat.

Wykgyl 1957

ON THE FANS

There were always crowds around Hogan. The galleries then were different than now — they were so much more respectful. There was always applause, not yelling like today. I miss the courteousness of the crowds back then and the dress as well.

For him to tip his cap, it was like someone else waving his arms or throwing a fist in the air.

■ *Westchester 1970*

EVERYONE PAID ATTENTION

Look at the attention that the fans are paying Hogan! Don Fairfield and Dan Sikes, his playing partners, the caddies... everybody watched Hogan when he played.

ONE OF A KIND

Hogan practiced setting himself apart, yet he had a great sense of humor when he got one-on-one. On the golf course, he could intimidate you, but he was really quite humble. He was very consistent. He was always the same. Great friends are always predictable.

■ *Westchester 1970*

ON PLAYING WITH HOGAN

When you played with Hogan he wouldn't talk much. It would have to be important. He rarely looked at you when you walked down the fairway. He always looked ahead. Sometimes we'd have a conversation and wouldn't look at each other. He was always planning, always concentrating.

He always had a reason to do something. Nothing was ever wasted.

■ *Westchester 1970*

GUIDELINES

In 1948 or 1949, several years before I met Hogan, I used two quotes by Ben as guidelines in developing my game:

□ "There isn't enough daylight in any one day to practice all the shots you need to practice."

□ "Every day you miss practicing, it will take you one day longer to be good."

■ *Westchester 1970*

■ *Westchester 1970*

AN INTERESTING COMBINATION

One time Hogan said, "If I had my game and Demaret's personality, I'd really be something."

A talent like this should live forever.

FINISHING ON TOP

Hogan stopped playing tournament golf on top, just like all of the great champions — Joe DiMaggio, Ted Williams, Rocky Marciano, and, of course, Byron Nelson, Bobby Jones, Babe Zaharias and Mickey Wright in golf. These were truly great athletes in their fields.